SUPERSTITION DIVERSITY

Superstitions, Witchcraft, Taboos, and Legends

Andrew Nyakupfuka

BALBOA.
PRESS
A DIVISION OF HAY HOUSE

ISBN: 978-1-4525-5999-5 (sc)
ISBN: 978-1-4525-5998-8 (e)

Balboa Press books may be ordered through booksellers or by contacting:

Balboa Press
A Division of Hay House
1663 Liberty Drive
Bloomington, IN 47403
www.balboapress.com
1-(877) 407-4847

Because of the dynamic nature of the Internet, any web addresses or links contained in this book may have changed since publication and may no longer be valid. The views expressed in this work are solely those of the author and do not necessarily reflect the views of the publisher, and the publisher hereby disclaims any responsibility for them.

The author of this book does not dispense medical advice or prescribe the use of any technique as a form of treatment for physical, emotional, or medical problems without the advice of a physician, either directly or indirectly. The intent of the author is only to offer information of a general nature to help you in your quest for emotional and spiritual well-being. In the event you use any of the information in this book for yourself, which is your constitutional right, the author and the publisher assume no responsibility for your actions.

Any people depicted in stock imagery provided by Thinkstock are models, and such images are being used for illustrative purposes only. Certain stock imagery © Thinkstock.

Printed in the United States of America

Balboa Press rev. date: 10/17/2012

I grew up in Zimbabwe's rural Mashonaland East province (Uzumba District) where superstition, legends, myths and witchcraft rule supreme. My grandmother told me a lot of folklore, some of which I failed to separate fiction from facts. I had to believe in those things as some of my friends were also told the same stories. We used to sit around a fire at night when these stories were narrated to us by the old grandmothers and grandfathers. My parents also believed in such stories such as witchcraft, superstitions, myths and taboos and they forced me to believe in them. For example we were told that animals, birds, and reptiles, trees, insects, and mountains used to talk. God used to communicate directly with his subjects, mountains used and fight on behalf the tribes around them. There is this funny story that Mount Zhombwe in Murehwa surrounded by the Zezuru tribe and Mount Mutemwa by the Buja tribe in Mutoko. These two tribes had an intense rivalry and they were always at war. One day these two mountains had a duel in support of their tribes .The duel took the whole day with their tribes cheering but none won the battle. Mount Mutemwa retreated to Mutoko town while Mount Zhombwe went to Murehwa town and they were separated by Nyadire River which acted as the umpire during the fight. We were told that there is spore which showed their movement of the mountains. I never saw the spore but we were told to believe the story without question. These two mountains are directly opposite each other as of today. Both mountains have granite summits. It is believed that the summits do have trees because of the fight. Native Americans had similar folklore to my people. Native Americans believed that birds, beasts, and reptiles had ears for human prayers, and endowed with influence on human destiny. They believed that lakes, rivers, waterfalls are sometimes the dwelling of place of the spirits. They further believe that lakes, rivers, and waterfalls have souls. Local people around Mount Nyanga in Zimbabwe believe the same as they think that Mount Nyanga has the ability to vanish people. As a child my grandmother told me that if I stood near a large pool of water, a crocodile could wrestle my shadow and I would fall into the pool and a crocodile could feast on. I therefore dreaded standing near such large bodies of water. She said that if a crocodile failed to wrestle my shadow, a mermaid would pull me down into that pool and it would feed me on worms, feces and mud, algae, rotten fish, and human flesh and many other dirty foods. It would release me after sometime and I would become a witch doctor or wizard. I was told that, time immemorial people used to ask God for some food under a "muhacha" tree and food would come as per their request. For example one could ask for rice and chicken and it would be provided. This is akin to manna from heaven in the Biblical story as Moses delivered the Israelites from bondage in Egypt.

Each country and culture has its superstations, taboos and myths. Some people believe in superstations and myths today. However, some people have been saved by natural science and modern religion and do not believe in such mysterious beliefs. It is my belief that people secretly believe in superstition, taboos and myths. The Free Merriam Dictionary defines superstation as a belief or practice resulting from ignorance, fear of the unknown, trust in magic or chance, or a false conception of causation or notion maintained despite evidence to the contrary. Myth can be referred to as traditional or legendary story, usually concerning some being or hero or event, with or without a determinable basis of fact or a natural explanation, especially one that is concerned with deities or demigods and explains some practice, rite, or phenomenon of nature. I am going to cite some superstition and myths from my rural Mashonaland East province and compare them with the same or similar beliefs in other parts of the world and show how mankind relate to each other in the global village. These will include: witchcraft, bizarre beliefs, folklore, taboos, and omens, lucky and unlucky things. The war of liberation in Zimbabwe unveiled some revolutionary legends in Zimbabwe like Chaminuka, Mbuya Nehanda, Sekuru Kaguvi, and many others. I will briefly touch on those and cite some further reading websites. There are some myths in Zimbabwe like, Nyaminyami, the River God, Mount Nyanga, where people could disappear without trace, and many others. I will also briefly touch on those.

Witchcraft

itches ride on Hyenas on their nefarious errands

Witch, in historical, anthropological, religious, and mythological, and contexts, is the use of alleged supernatural or magical powers. Zimbabweans in general believe in witchcraft, though some pretend that witchcraft does not exist. Witches

A Witch on a Mission

and wizards are believed to be agents of the devil. It is believed that witchcraft runs in certain families and could be inherited. Some

Hyena: Witchcraft Transportation Merchant.

people believe that some people actually buy some witchcraft apparatus like goblins (zvikwambo/tokoloshis) to enhance their business performance or to destroy their adversaries or foes. It is a common belief that witches and wizards are cannibals. They use some magic to exhume the corpses, hence sons-in-law in my local area have to put up at the grave of a recently deceased to protect the corpse from the witches and wizards. It is common to hear young witchcraft apprentices talk about visiting certain families in the wake of the night or eating human flesh. Just like in other cultures witches and wizards use broom sticks, hyenas, jackals and other people, and baskets as transportation tools. New Zimbabwe.com reported a story in Murehwa where a witch travelled about seventy-five miles in winnowing basket for the sole purpose of witchcraft. For more information about this story go to the following websites, http://www.newzimbabwe.com/pages/witchcraft7.19898.html. http://www.iol.co.za/news/africa/naked-witches-to-face-trial-1.1330309

It is believed that witchcraft is active during the night and the witches will be naked. This confirms the prevalence of witchcraft in Zimbabwe. There is also a town called Karoi (witch) in Zimbabwe's Mashonaland West Province. This city has a broomstick on its logo further proving that witchcraft is a popular trade. As a young boy I was told that some witches/wizards use snakes in their craft to leak on the bodies of their victims at night so that they suffer from ill health similar to malnutrition. It is believed that these snakes are kept in large clay pots where they are dressed in beads and fed on mealie meal. I could not verify this assertion as we were told never to go near a neighbor's granary where the snake was kept. Some witches/wizards are believed to use some magical missiles (nyanga)to

Lifeless Goblin: Goblins could be in the forms of stone or wooden scultures.

strike their victims. The missiles are filled with some black magic. There is a region in Zimbabwe called Nyanga where people of bad intentions used to go and buy these missiles.

Goblins are not confined to miniature humans but animals like baboons, rabbits, dogs and many others. Goblins could also be in the form of lifeless objects like the stone sculpture shown above. Goblins can talk. They can be send on errands to demand some services on behalf of their masters. It is believed that male goblins could be problematic as they may demand to have sex with their masters' wives or daughters. If that demand is not met they can cause irreparable damage to the master which may result in death. It is further believed that most Zimbabweans buy their goblins from South Africa.

Witchcraft is not only confined to black magic but may be used for peaceful purposes. Many Zimbabweans believe that both males and females can use love potions to enhance their families. Love potions are administered to the partner without their knowledge. A love potion is designed to enshrine another's feelings using magic. It is believed that anyone who prescribes a love potion is either a witch/wizard or an accomplice. Some people enlist the services of a witch doctor (n'anga) to prescribe a love potion. There is a very thin line between a witch/wizard and a witch doctor (n'anga/sangoma) as both parties engage in black magic although a witch doctor prescribes medicine to the sick who could have been bewitched.

People in Zimbabwe seek counsel from witch doctors (n'anga/sangoma) or prophets to sniff out witches and wizards from their families. Witch doctors use some black magic to protect the homes of the afflicted witch craft victims. It is believed that the magic may turn the home of the intended victim into an imaginary large pool of water at night. When the witch comes they see a large pool of water and may not find the victim. Some people have some magic to catch the witches if they come to their homes. If they catch a witch they may insert a forked stick into the anus of the witch and rapture the colon or hammer in a six inch nail in the center of the skull. It is believed that witches do not cry or wince during the ordeal. They do not die at the crime scene but die in the comfort of their homes. It is said that witch doctors could conduct a daylight witch hunt at the invitation of a village head or chief. It is believed that the accused or suspected witches would be given a concoction. If they do not throw out or suffer from diarrhea that was confirmation that they were either a witch or wizard. They were burnt alive on a pyre of freshly cut logs starting from the legs up to the head. That was a slow and painful death. The capital punishment was designed to deter would be witches/wizards to relinquish the trade. Most countries meted capital punishment to convicted witches. The United States is no exception. There is a detailed history of witchcraft under the title: The Salem Witchcraft Trials of 1692.To read more visit the following website; http://law2.umkc.edu/faculty/projects/ftrials/salem/salem.htm Countries like France, Mexico, and Germany, Scotland, South Africa, and Italy and others have verifiable lists of those executed. The lists include names and dates. To get a detailed overview of the Burning Times, go to the following website; http://www.witchway.net/times/times.html South Africa prosecuted and convicted nine (9) witches as late as between 1998 to 1999.Witches could face the hangman or a jail sentence besides burning. Witchcraft in China is deeply entrenched in elements of mysticism, religion and art. Chinese witchcraft employs books, staffs, and other implements, as well as rabbits, which are traditionally associated with the moon and with occult matters. In Japan the shamanistic religion Shinto has always been widely accepted in conjunction with Buddhism. The Japanese never attached negative connotations to witchcraft, and the word "witch" may often be used with positive connotation in Japanese language.

"Mukutu" is a New Zealand Maori word meaning witchcraft, sorcery, or spell or incantation. Witchcraft was apparently prominent in pre-European times, although there have been sporadic modern references to "mukutu", curses, and exorcisms. India is no exception to witchcraft. Indians believe in witchcraft especially those in the lower social and economic stratum. It is the poor women, the old, and widows who are falsely accused, persecuted, and convicted of witchcraft. Witchdoctors play the witch hunt role. Those convicted in the witchcraft, "kangaroo courts" face dehumanizing punishment such as being paraded naked, beaten black and blue by the villagers. Their hair and tongues can be chopped off, banished from the village after severe punishment like hanging on a tree upside down and whipped. Some perceived witches face capital punishment through burning. Their teeth can be plucked out or hands and legs can be broken or forced to eat excreta. You can read more about the penalties witches face in India on the following website: http://www.newstrackindia.com/newsdetails/3032

The British colonial government put in place the Witchcraft Suppression Act in Southern Rhodesia, making it criminal to accuse someone of practicing the trade. However, the Zimbabwe Government made some amendments to the colonial law in July 2006 .The amendment stipulates that witchcraft will be a criminal offence punishable by a fine or a five-year jail term. You can read more about this amendment on the following website http://www.newzimbabwe.com/pages/witchcraft2.14064.html

Traditional healers are still a part of everyday life in Zimbabwe. They are a much respected component of society are regulated by). ZINATHA (Zimbabwe National Traditional Healers Association).

Superstitions
Dreams

Dreams play an important role in the world of superstition. People always have dreams but may not know the meaning of their dreams. The American Heritage Dictionary defines a dream as a series of images, ideas, emotions, and sensations occurring involuntarily in the mind during certain stages of sleep. If you are a Christian you very well know the Biblical dream of the Pharaoh in Egypt. He dreamt about seven fat and seven lean cows. The seven lean cows devoured the

A Black Cat: Condemned in many cultures as an agent of bad luck.

seven fat cows. Pharaoh's prophets or sorcerers failed to interpret the dream but Joseph was able to. Dreams have got different interpretations according to one's region of residence or culture. I have selected a few dreams from my original region of residence in Zimbabwe; even in Zimbabwe the selected dreams have different meanings. You may find some similarities in these selected dreams in your culture.

If one dreams of:

- A white wedding it means that there is going to be a death in the family. Zimbabweans wrap their dead in a white cloth. Americans further believe that if you dream of cats attacking you represent enemies; if you succeed banishing them you will overcome obstacles and rise in fortune and fame.

- Rainy day. It means there is peace in the family or in the community. Water is a sign of life. Americans and other cultures believe that to dream of rain is generally considered as a good omen unless the rain falls on cattle, for this means a business loss of some kind. Rain usually represents cleansing and purification. It can also represent the release of tension that comes after the storm or a period of crying. (Note the song: I Can See Clearly Now by Johnny Nash).Rain replenishes and brings fertility so it may also symbolizes that you are opening to a new phase of personal growth in your life.

  Source: Rain Dream Meaning -
  http://www.dreamsleep.net/rain-dream-meaning.html

- Catching some fish. It means you are going to receive some money from someone. The Chinese perceive fish represent the calm and wisdom of God. It means that you have to keep yourself near the dictates of God and never do what is wrong. The Chinese further believe that this means that you are going to "fish" someone you desire, a treasure from the bottom of the sea, something really special! This is an excellent dream message, and I really hope that you'll see many dreams where you are catching fish or watching them calmly and silently swim. Article Source: http://EzineArticles.com/1912613

- A black cat. It means an unfortunate omen, for example a death in the family or something really bad is going to happen to you like a car accident or a serious injury. Black cats are associated with witches. Do not engage in gambling as a black cat denotes bad lucky. Americans believe that dreaming of a black cat is generally unfortunate omen and it shows treachery as well as a run of bad luck. Cats attacking you represent enemies; if you succeed banishing them you will overcome great obstacles and rise in fortune and fame. Most cultures black cats may indicate magical happenings, or bad luck depending on your personal beliefs, while white cats may symbolize protection and blessings. http://www.gotohoroscope.com/txt/dream-interpretation-cat.html

- An Owl. It means that witches or wizards were in your bedroom that night or they are planning to visit you. You better visit a witch doctor "n'anga/sangoma" for counsel and guidance or protection. Native Americans attributed owls with wisdom and sacred knowledge. The shaman would call upon Owl medicine for insight into the truth of ill –intent. Plains Indians wore owl feathers to themselves against evil spirits. Many cultures view the owl in high esteem. They associate the owl with the following attributes: intelligence, brilliance, and wisdom, power, knowledge, and intuition, messages, mysticism and, mystery, unconscious and, silent observation, independence, and protection, bravery, and transition, longevity and, reincarnation, and many others. The Chinese consider the owl as inauspicious. They believe that the hooting is an expression of digging a grave. The Mandarin perceives the word "owl" is synonymous with killing a person and placing his head on a pole. Chinese farmers consider the owl as a pest control as they eat rodents which destroy their crops. Europeans in general also view an owl in bad light. They also believe that if an owl hoots on top of your house, it means someone is going to die. If it hoots in a field or forest, it is predicted that the future brings bad time.

- Funeral procession or vigil. It means that there is going to be a new arrival- a birth in the family. But if you dream of a birth it means the opposite. There is going to be a death. Some believe that dreaming of attending a funeral

An Owl. Perceived Witchcraft Courier

ceremony is a sign of your need to accept some kind of loss in order to move on. It is a good omen that will dispel bad luck and brings good luck. It can transform misfortune into good fortune.

- Dogs barking and running all over your yard. It means that they are chasing away intruders like ghosts, witches, and wizards. Generally, if you dream about dogs it is a good omen as the dog is our best friend. The western world believes that if a dog howls, death is near. They believe that dogs can detect evil. In Scotland, they believe that a strange dog coming to the house means a new friendship. The British on the other hand it is good luck to see a spotted dog on your way to work.

- Dream of deceased relatives. Be careful, they are inviting you to the world of the dead. But if they are friendly to you, they do not want you to join them. Americans believe that dreaming of a deceased person and this person speaks to only you, pay attention to what the spirit is telling you as it could be very important to you.

- A lot of lice in your hair and you are wearing torn clothes. It is a good omen; you are going to be wealthy in future. This adds up to the adage, from rags to riches.

- Plushy orchard. This is a good omen. If you are looking for a job you are going to get a rewarding job. However, some cultures have their superstitions on individual fruits. Nikki Phipps (2007) a Yahoo Contributor Network on, More Gardening Superstitions: Fruit and Veggie Tales, came up with some interesting observations on some fruits. She said that fruit has been associated with love and marriage, and fortune telling. Her assertion concurs with my folks on a dream on a plushy orchard. Phipps says that some in cultures, dead animals are buried with newly planted fruit trees to ensure good harvests. The first crop of cherries is sometimes given to women who have recently given birth. It is believed that this ritual will ensure an abundant harvest. The pits (or stones) of cherries are said to foretell marriage. Phipps goes on to say that do not walk through an orchard without wiping your feet with a cherry leaf, lest you are sure to choke on a cherry pit. Phipps says that peaches are a symbol of long life and responsible for warding off evil spirits. She also came up with the bad side of fruit. Some people believe that menstruating women coming into contact with any fruit or veggie will spoil the entire crop. Some people believe that the apple tree is a bad omen if it blossoms during the fall or leave a single apple on the tree during harvest season. She says that apples play prominent roles in many Halloween traditions from bobbing for apples to apple cider and candied apples. For more information visit the following website:http://voices.yahoo.com/more-gardening-superstitions-fruit-veggie-tales-519285.html?cat=32

- Falling from a tree or moving vehicle. This is a bad omen. You may be fired or laid off from your job. Americans believe that to dream of falling indicates a loss of emotional equilibrium or self control. It may represent your insecurity, or a lack of self confidence, a fear of failure or an inability to cope with a situation. If you fall a long distance in your dream and get hurt, be prepared for really hard times ahead; but if you fall and not injured your upsets will be minor and temporary.

- Pregnant woman. It means there is going to be a renewal of things in your life or you may get a new job. Pregnancy symbolizes change or development in your current status. It may mean promotion at your job place. You may receive very important visitors you have never met before.

- An inferno. This signifies bad luck. You are going to lose most of your wealth or property. However, Craig Hamilton-Parker (1999) says that fire represents the process of psychological transformation. A fire destroys but it also cleanses and purifies. It can cause pain. Therefore dreaming of fire can signal a new beginning, spiritual illumination, sexual passion or disruptive emotions such as the flames of passion or envy. http://www.dreamsleep.net/meaning-of-fire-dream.html

- Puddle of dirty water. It means that some people would ruin whatever you are trying to do. Other cultures believe that murky water represents unpleasantness will go with you for a few rounds. It is further suggested to wet your feet into the puddle foretells that your pleasure will work you harm afterwards. However, believe that clear water is a sign of good lucky, a dream of muddy water foretells sadness or sorry for the dreamer through hearing of an illness or death of someone he/she knows very well. http://www.experienceproject.com/dream-dictionary/Puddle-dreams

- Twitch in your eyes. Twitch in the right eye means you are going to be happy and twitch in the left eye means sorrow. Americans believe that a twitch in the left eye signifies that there will be a death in the family. Indians however, believe that an itch in the eye means that someone is maligning you, or you envy someone.

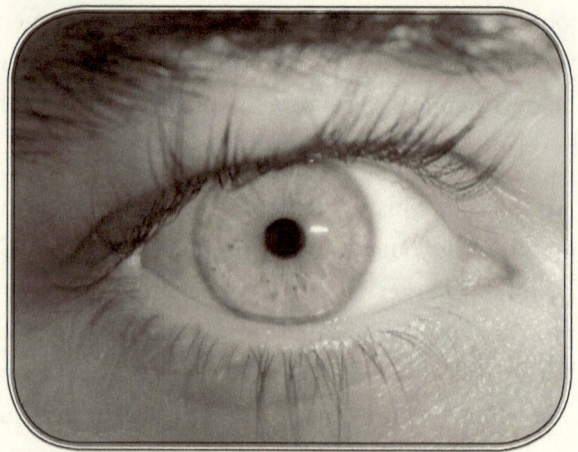

Twitch in the Eye

- Baboon/Monkey. My original local area of residence is a haven baboons and monkeys. Dreaming about baboons/monkeys is is a good omen. It represents a direct communication with your spiritual ancestors .It means you are blessed and your foes will be driven away. It is a sign of prosperity. Americans believe that to dream of a monkey denotes that you have deceitful friends who will flatter you to advance their interests.

- Swept by a current of water. My local people believe that a current of water symbolizes failure in what you are planning to achieve. For students it signifies failure in examinations. Business people dread dreaming about a current of water as it is a sign of their business empire. For lovers it means the relationship is going to fail. My local people also believe that failing to cross a river with strong current is akin to dream falling off the roof of a building or cliff. They speculate that you are through some difficult times and you are afraid of what is ahead of you. However, Holloway Gillian in her excerpt: "Water in Your Dreams", says that the necessity to cross a river is often symbolic of a phase that you must move through prior to achieving the goal you are after, or as part of digesting a past experience. However, failing to cross a river is a chilling forecast as you will not be successful. It is also believed that a strong current of water is only a warning of some things to come your way good or bad. The Chinese believe that if you dream about a broken bridge it means you are going to face some lawsuits or alternatively if you dream about a high tide, instead of a strong current of water it is a sign of prosperity.

Some changes in the environment may signify some consequences or rewards to the community, for example:

- If a tree in your yard wilts and eventually dies. This means one of your parents or head of a household will get sick and eventually die.

- If the bamboos within your community wilt and eventually die. It means the chief will get sick and die. The Chinese have a similar dream though with a different meaning. The Chinese believe that if you dream about bamboos growing healthy in you your yard, that there will be some good news coming your way.

- Pointing at a grave using your second finger means that finger will be rigid and will not be flexible. You have to point at a grave using your small finger. The Chinese have a similar superstition which states that never point at the moon or your ears might get chopped off. Indians have a different version from the Chinese dream about the moon. Indians believe that if you dream about the moon, you are going to meet a lady or it is a sign in business fortune

- Sitting on the middle of the road. It means you are going to suffer from boils. The superstition is meant to educate people on the dangers of being run over by cars. There is also a belief that if you have boils use a coin to remove the puss and put the coin at the cross roads. Whoever, picks up the coin will be afflicted with boils and you are cured. Hence people in my area of residence do not pick up anything they see at crossroads as it may bring bad luck.

- If a young man eats from a cooking pot it means they are going to be gay/impotent or they are going to develop some breasts like women. In my culture men do not cook or prepare food. That is the responsibility for women.

- If a pregnant woman sees a baboon, monkey or any other animal, she will give birth to a child who will have the characteristics of that particular animal. To avoid that she should spit at that animal and sulk. African Americans believe that do not go to the zoo when you are pregnant. I think they perceive the same consequences as a pregnant African woman in my local area of residence. The Chinese believe that if you strike an animal during pregnancy, the new born child will look like that animal and behave like that animal.

- Twitch under your feet. It means you are going to step on dung or human feces. Most rural boys in Zimbabwe do not put on shoes. Most of them are herd boys.

Americans believe that if the bottom of your right foot itches, you are going to take a trip.

- If an owl hoots on top of your house or hut, it means the witches are nearby or something bad is going to befall your family.

- Swarms of army worms on the onset of summer spell means an impending drought.

- Women and girls of reproductive age do not brew beer for the ancestral spirits as they are considered unclean. The ritual beer is brewed by young girls under the age of ten and very old women who long have ceased sexual intercourse and they no longer go for their monthly periods. This fits well with an Indian belief that menstruating women are regarded unclean and are isolated. They cannot enter the kitchen till they are "clean "again.

- Hear a jackal howl in the morning or evening near your village. It means there is going to be a death in the village especially if someone is sick. Jackals, hare, and wolves are considered evil. It is perceived that witches use these animal as merchants of death. The Chinese however believe that hearing a crow between the hours of three and seven means gifts are on the way. Indians believe that a howling of a dog at night chills the blood as it is a portent of death approaching.

- If the wind blows from west to east, that is a sign of the onset of a rain season. Normally wind blows from east to west in other seasons. However, Indians believe that the cooing of a bird or dove heralds the advent of spring. The Chinese believe that hanging wind chimes near your home will bring wealth and prosperity to you and your family. However, some Chinese believe that wind chimes scare away evil spirits when hung in doorways and windows can dissuade bad luck from entering a home. But in older days, people believed that hanging wind chimes in your home will attract naughty spirits. http://milkasue.blogspot.com/2010/10/chinese-superstition-wind-chimes.html

- If boys eat cooked dried pumpkin leaves in summer they will develop leprosy. Pumpkin leaves are a seasonal relish; therefore it should not be eaten in the next season. It is believed that it is not good at all. In any case women used to dispose of it. Girls did not enjoy it although it was said that no disease would affect them. I noticed that men had an excellent appetite for meat hence they discouraged boys to eat the dried pumpkin leaves in the off season. They encouraged boys to go out hunting. Indians have their own taboos on a variety of foods. Indians believe that if you do not crush the egg shells after having the egg they will be gathered by a witch who will then use the shells to make a boat for herself. Thus if you crushed the shells, they would be of no use to her. Indians further believe that if you come a across a hole in a loaf of bread that you cut, it stands for a coffin and means that someone will die soon. It is rather strange since most loaves of baked bread have some holes in them. Indians also believe that all loaves of bread must be marked with a sign of a cross before baking. The intention was to thwart the devil from sitting on the loaf and spoiling the bread. The food taboos among the Chinese general public have much to do with seasonal characteristics. Meaning that diet must change as the season change. The same kind of food is fitting for a certain time but not for the rest. The Chinese had their version of seasonal vegetables. They believed that having leek in winter and spring can "warm the back of the knee."However, in summer, leek makes people "dizzy" with poor vision. Dog meat is a really tasty treat during wintertime, but should be avoided in other seasons. Fresh hot peppers are loved by the people in Jiangxi Province in the summer. For the winter, dried hot peppers can still be had. But for autumn, basically no hot peppers are in the daily diet. http://www.bellaonline.com/ArticlesP/art177134.asp

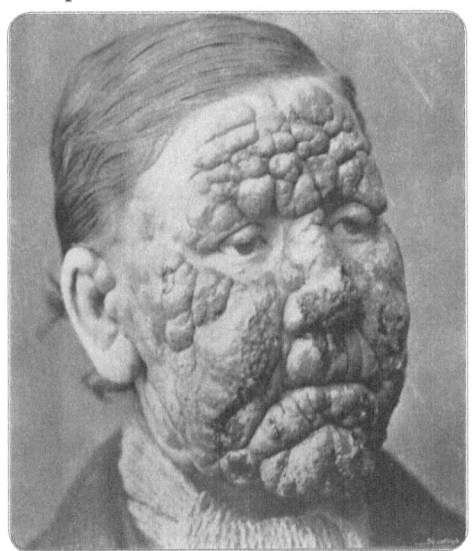

Leper: Eating off -season dried pumpkin leaves could cause leprosy.

The Moon. My people believe that the different phases of the moon cause or aggravates mental disturbance on those people who are insane, who suffer from epilepsy, leprosy, and women on periods, those who have medical procedures. It is believed that there is resurgence of ailments at particular phases of the moon. The afflicted people need particular attention and monitoring or medication. People from the developed world believe that the full moon causes mental disturbance and criminal tendencies. The moon has been accused of disturbing the minds of men since ancient times. In ancient Greece and Rome it was also the occasion of a bacchanalia which was a classical name for a drunken outdoor party. The Lunar Effect theory speculates that crime and hospital admissions rise during the full moon. However, some people believe that the moon is a symbol of the feminine and is also associated with love and romance. A bright, full moon foretells good fortune and prosperity. It signifies that there are many pleasant things ahead and that you will expect good fortune.

- Beating a boy with a broom will make him a coward or he will always be in the company of woman. Alternatively he will never marry. Any boy who befriends women is regarded lazy a social outcast. The Chinese on the other hand believe that beating a person with broom will bring bad luck to that person for years. The western world believes that you do not lean a broom against a bed; evil spirit will cast a spell on the bed. Westerners also believe that if you sweep rubbish out of a door after dark, a stranger will visit. My local people also believe that you do not throughout the rubbish you sweep at night. If you do you are throwing out the riches which are on your way. Westerners believe that if someone sweeps over your feet you will never get married. Never take an old broom to a new house. There is also a belief in the USA that if a young girl steps over a broom handle she will become a mother before she becomes a wife.

Hunters or fishermen do not eat okra. It is believed that animals would slip away from them like the texture of cooked okra.However, Burros M.(1986) in her article in New York Times News Service believes otherwise. She believes in the American superstition which speculates that if you do not eat okra you do not catch fish. She supports the eating of fruit as healthy. She believes in the American adage, "Feed a cold and starve a fever- an apple a day keeps the doctor away."You can read more about Marian Burros' line of thinking on the following website: http://articles. sun-sentinel.com/1986-07-23/features/8602130068_1_hot-water-spinach-fever However, there is no logical thinking in superstitions. The world's most beautiful women Cleopatra of Egypt and Yang Guifei of China loved okra and included okra in their diets, while Japan's old and young from rural Kami in Kowchi Prefecture had beautiful smiles. They believed that such smiles came from eating okra.

Girls do not eat the adder of a cow. If they eat, they will develop breast cancer.

- If you walk backwards you could be eaten by a lion.

- Children do eat eggs as they would develop epilepsy.

- A bounty of wild fruits signifies a good season with adequate rain.

- If your palms are twitching, it means you are going to receive money from someone or someone is going to give you a gift. African Americans have a similar superstition. They believe that if your palm is itching it means you are coming into some money.

- The widow of a deceased person should wear a black outfit and head gear for a year to show sorrow and sadness over the death of the spouse. She should also cut her hair from time to time within that period. The children of the deceased should also cut their hair from time to time within the year. The widower should also sew on a black piece of cloth on his sleeve to show the same. The Chinese have a similar practice. They believe that the deceased children and grandchildren should cut their hair for forty-nine days. Indians believe that if there is a death in the family, family members are considered unclean and they should not go to the temple until the stipulated period is over.

- Seeing a rabbit or buck crossing the road ahead when you are on a journey means bad luck. You have to back home. Indians believe to the contrary. They believe seeing an elephant when one is leaving for a journey is considered good luck. This is because an elephant represents Lord Ganesha, the Indian God who is the harbinger of good luck and removes all obstacles. North Americans believe that if a black cat crosses your path you will have bad luck during the day.

- Knocking on Wood. The British and Americans believe that knock three times on wood after speaking of good fortune, or bad luck will ruin it; the phrase "touch wood" is used for luck in Britain and Ireland, even when there is no wood nearby. Local people in my area of residence do not have anything to do with knocking on wood. However, they dread a certain tree species called "muparamhosva" (lit. commit a crime) as firewood for cooking or for warming themselves in the courtyard. The "muparamhosva" timber was not even considered for huts or barn construction because of the stigma I have alluded to. It is believed using the "muparamhosva" wood will condemn you to committing a crime which would take you to the chief's court. We used to cut down the "muparamhosva on sight" because we did not want to commit crimes which would take us to the chief's court or magistrate's court. Our parents never discouraged us from the wanton destruction of the tree, they actually encouraged us. The "muparamhosva" tree has no commercial value. I discovered that the "muparamhosva" firewood burned very slowly and it produced a bad smell. I am sure that is why that the tree was condemned. Many ancient pagan European rituals involved the spirits of sacred trees, especially oak, ash, holly, hawthorn and yew. The pagans believed that trees housed spirits, and touching the trees in respectful manner encouraged the spirits to grant health and prosperity. Christians believed the wood symbolizes the timber of the True Cross of Christ's crucifixion.

Elephant: An omen of good luck in India.

If your ear drum is vibrating. It means someone is talking about you. African Americans believe the same. Indians on the other hand believe that hiccups indicate someone is thinking about you.

- Seeing a Chameleon brings bad luck while the sight of a lizard signifies good luck. As a young boy, my friends and I used to hunt for chameleons and kill them so that we won't be unlucky. It was believed that the chameleon condemned humans to permanent death while the lizard assured humans that if humans die, they will resurrect one day. Therefore the chameleon was viewed evil. West Africans and many parts of Africa dread chameleons as well. In the pre- Christian time, Chameleons were believed to be sacred to the sun, and it was said that they never had to eat it. Later Christian missionaries in Africa associated chameleons with the devil- who could change his appearance to deceive mankind – they have been stuck with that reputation ever since. Lizards have a better reputation. In ancient Egypt they represented divine wisdom and good fortune. They were revered as gods by the people of the Pacific Islands.

Taboos

The Free Encyclopedia defines a taboo as a vehement prohibition of an action based on the belief that such behavior is either too sacred or too accursed for ordinary individuals to undertake, under threat of supernatural punishment. I have selected a few taboos in local area of residence in Zimbabwe. These selected taboos are not representative of Zimbabwe taboos but somehow there are some similarities. Some of the taboos have been overtaken by western civilizations. But some people still believe in some of them. Each of them has a cultural value. Below are some of the taboos I have selected:

- Eating the meat from an animal related to your totem may result in you losing all your teeth. For example my totem is Lion (Shumba) it means I do eat meat from all members of the cat family or meat from any animal killed by members of the cat family.

- Women of reproductive age and girls do not smoke cigarettes or any tobacco products and drink beer unless if they are prostitutes or women past menopause. This is a moral and health issue. It is believed that young women might affect their yet to be born children as nicotine is hazardous to their health. Alcohol makes one lose their moral values. Please note; young men and boys are prohibited from smoking and drinking for the same reasons. However, this taboo is losing the battle to western values.

- Calling your parents by their first names. You only address them as dad (baba/amai) or mother. This is a matter of respect. It took me a while to know my father's name.

- Fathers and their sons do not take a bath together or share a shower but mothers and their daughters can. This is a matter of respect as male reproductive organs are exposed. It is considered disrespectful to see your father's private parts.

- Fathers and sons do not eat from the same plate while mothers and their daughters can. Please note that it is a common practice for people of the same age or social strata to eat from one plate. The belief is that people who eat from the same plate will not betray each other. View MOB eating on YouTube video on the following website: http://www.youtube.com/watch?v=h_4MCKL6kcg

The Chinese believe that instead of having food served from individual plates, the Chinese eat from one a common dish in the middle of a round table or from several dishes placed on a large lazy susan on round table. Diners are expected to place food on a small or on a bowl of rice in front of them but often they plunge their chopsticks into a shared dish and eat straight from that. When eating the Chinese reach across one another, pass dishes, pour each other drinks and put food on each other's plate. It is an Indian custom to wash the hands and feet thoroughly before consuming a meal, since Indians are accustomed to eating on the floor. A traditional family meal is first served to the male members, with the head of the family being served first. Women eat only after the rest of the family has dined.

- Cousins do not marry. (Makunakuna)If this happens the culprits will be prosecuted at the chief's banished from the district or they pay a white heifer as a fine to the chief. The Chinese believe that couples with the same surname should not marry, even if they are not related, they still belong to the same ancestry.

- It is taboo for Zimbabweans to marry in the month of November. If one breaks the taboo they will be prosecuted and fined by the chief. The perpetrator my pay an unspecified number of cattle goats and pieces of cloth. The fines vary among different chiefs. If one defies paying the fine it is believed that the ancestral spirits will punish the perpetrator. It is believed that members of his family may die mysteriously or may have hallucinations; his animals may be killed by lions, hyenas, and leopards or crocodiles. His crops may be destroyed by baboons. The perpetrator may meet with different kind bad luck. Lately one of the deputy prime ministers in Zimbabwe breached the marriage taboo. He was summoned to the chief's court but defied the summons and was convicted in absentia. He had to go through the government courts where he was exonerated of any wrong doing.

- Husband and wife do not kiss or embrace each other in public. It is believed that kissing in public is a sign of promiscuity. Kissing and hugging is confined to the bedroom. It is a private affair. Most rural folks do not kiss .However, with time this taboo is slowly fading away. But I am yet to see rural unsophisticated folks kiss in public. There are other cultures which do not kiss at all. The Somalis do not kiss at all in public or privately. In ancient China, kissing is considered being on par with coitus, and thus kissing was confined to the bedroom. Some Chinese believe in Confucius. Confucius had taught that the process of attaining perfection as a human being is to suppress all emotional display. So no touch, no verbal praise, not even a blatant look of pleasure. As result, children brought up in Confucian tradition consciously or unconsciously imbibe in the notion that it is inappropriate to show any feelings no matter how sad or happy. In strict Muslim countries public kissing is prohibited. In Vietnam, spouses do kiss outside the home and not in front of their children. Parents rarely kiss their children. The western world through the ancient Greek civilization believes there is nothing wrong in kissing in public. The British believe that kissing under the branch of mistletoe will lead to marriage. The mistletoe was considered sacred and was admired because of its ability to grow in oak trees. The mistletoe was considered sacred by the ancient Greek and its link with kissing is reported to come from them. The Norse mythology is different from the Greeks. They believed that after the misadventure involving Loki and the death of god Baldr, mistletoe was appointed as a sacred plant of peace; thereafter any enemies who met beneath mistletoe were obliged to lay their arms and keep a truce until the next day. The Chinese believe that if you dream standing underneath a tree not necessarily a mistletoe tree it means help from powerful people. Indians believe that giving a kiss signifies some good deeds.

- You do not eat meat from an animal or chicken which died on its own. We do not burn the meat but give it to dogs. We preserve what is left for future dog consumption. We believe that animal or chicken should be properly slaughtered. The slaughtered animal should shed some blood. We believe that an animal has got a soul and the soul is in its blood. We use an ax to chop the animal at the back of its neck and a sharp knife to cut off the neck of a chicken. However, some men eat the blood of an animal which comes from the back of the head. They mix the blood with some pieces of offal like small intestines, lungs, pancreas, an others and boil them. Women of reproductive age and girls are prohibited from eating the boiled blood. The belief being that they may have problems with their monthly periods. We do not eat chicken blood. Animals which die on their own are considered dirty. We believe that if an animal is sick or has an accident in the pastures we have to slaughter it in the proper way so that we will be able to eat its meat. However, due to the scarcity of meat some people eat those animals which die on their own. I have witnessed some people being treated for anthrax. Our original taboo of not eating animals and chickens which die on unknown reasons confirms very well with Judaism, Christianity, and Islam. Moslems follow strictly the following quote in the Koran, "Allah has forbidden you what dies of itself (Maytata), and blood, and the flesh of swine, and that is which is slaughtered as a sacrifice over which any other name than that of Allah has been invoked(or has been slaughtered for idols, etc which Allah's Name has not been mentioned while slaughtered. But whoever is driven by necessity, without neither willful disobedience nor transgressing due limits, then he is guiltless. Surely Allah is Oft-forgiving, merciful." (2:173. Schrrimacher T. (1995), gave the following reading verses on his thesis: The Biblical Prohibition from Eating Blood), why Jews and Christians should not eat, blood, animals not properly slaughtered and for sacrifices purposes. Genesis9: 4-5; Leviticus 7:26-27; 17: 10-12; 14; 19:26. Deuteronomy 14:21. These Biblical verses prohibit the eating of blood. The following verse gives an accurate account of why Jews, Christians and Moslems should not eat animals slaughtered for sacrifice purposes; Leviticus 3:17.The last Biblical verses explains why Christians and Jews should not eat animals not properly slaughtered; Exodus 22:30; Leviticus 17 :15 ;Leviticus 17 :15 ; Deuteronomy 14 :21 ; Acts 15:19-20. For more information visit the following website: http://www.contra-mundum.org/schirrmacher/eating_blood.pdf

- Eat Calf/Veal. It is taboo for my people eat meat from a calf. Those who have eaten calf meat said that the meat is tasteless and disgusting. Those who ate veal are ridiculed and isolated .They are seen as anti-culture, outcasts anti-social, or gluttons. Calves are never, ever, slaughtered and those which die for unknown reasons

Calf: It is taboo to eat veal or any
young one of any animal.

are given to dogs, burned, or buried. Slaughtering calves is tantamount to reducing one's herd. Ancestral spirits abhor the practice. It actually never happens. However, the west eats calf meat/veal. There are five different types of veal namely Bob veal, Formula –Fed veal, and Non-Formula fed veal, Rose veal, and Free veal. Bob veal comes from calves that are slaughtered when they are a few days to a month old and they weigh about sixty (60) pounds. The Formula-Fed veal comes from 18-20 weeks old calves. The calves are raised on milk formula supplement. The meat color is ivory or creamy pink, with a firm, fine and velvet appearance. Non -Formula- fed veal comes from calves 22-26 weeks old, fed on grain, hay, or other food, in addition to milk. The meat is darker in color and some marbling fat may be apparent. Rose veal is from calves 35 weeks old. These calves are raised in the United Kingdom. The last type is the Free veal which comes from 24weeks old calves which are raised in the pastures, and have unlimited access to their mothers' milk and pastures. They are not administered hormones and antibiotic.

Veal is a good source of Protein, Niacin, Riboflavin, Vitamin B6, Vitamin B12, Phosphorus and Zinc. Veal is also high in Cholesterol. Veal contains very little fat, not more than 10 grams of fat per 100 grams, many of them unsaturated fats and because of this, veal is considered very lean. Veal has many advantages. It is a valuable source of nutrients; it is tender, lean, digested easily and above all – just delicious.

Luster, J.M. (2012) and some animal activists have the perception of veal as fundamentally cruel arose during a period when the veal industry was focused on a product they called "milk fed" veal also known as "white" veal. In order to maintain tenderness and a white color to the meat calves were crated so they could barely move and fed a low-iron milk replacement diet. Hundreds of immobile calves, in crates with slatted wooden floors so that the manure, which was basically liquid could just fall though to the floor, it was only hosed out of the barn when they changed over the animals, the stench is amazing.

http://www.quora.com/Meat/Is-veal-production-crueler-than-with-other-forms-of-meat

There is a common saying, Do Chinese eat veal, and Of course we eat anything with four legs, except a table."Indians do not eat veal for religious reasons. They cannot eat veal while they do not eat the cow.

Husband and wife do show their love passion in the presence of their children.

- Mothers in-law and sons in-law do not shake hands or embrace, the same with fathers in-law and daughters in-law. They always keep a reasonable distance from each other.

- Boys do not sit on a grinding stone .If they do, it is believed they will become impotent or bald.

- You do not mend or sew garment while wearing it. My local people believe that if you mend a garment while wearing it is a sign of bad luck. They believe your problems will stick with forever. The Chinese believe that to mend clothes while wearing them is always unfortunate. In some districts it is said to be a death omen, in others a sign that mender will make enemies, or come to want. In mending, as in dressmaking, the use of black or dark thread on light-colored materials is unlucky. When putting on new clothes for the first time, the mender is usually advised to make a wish. If there is a pocket, a coin should be put into at once, to ensure plenty of money whilst wearing the coat or use dress in future. Children appearing in new clothes are often pinched by their friend.

- Charms. (Dumwa) My local people believe in love and luck charms. These charms are usually prescribed by a witchdoctor (n'anga" or any other person who has knowledge in the love and lucky charms. A witchdoctor prescribes some herbs which you will mix with some facial oils so that girls or boys see you as handsome, beautiful or favorably. The intention is that your star shines better than others. The witchdoctor can give you some herbs which you put in your bathing water but you do use bathing soap so that you wash away all the bad luck. If you are looking for a job the employer will see you favorably. You can use the same charms when going to court. The prosecutor and the judge may acquit you even though you committed the crime.

The witchdoctor can sew some herbs in a black piece of cloth which you may wear as an arm band but under your sleeve. You can also use the charm when gambling. Some modern love charms come in the form of necklaces, rings, and bracelets or anklets The Chinese also believe in charms, charms are mandates (orders), issued under the seal and painted with a cinnabar pencil. They are the principal means of commanding spectres, expelling and killing "Kwei –Evil Spirits". They help to catch, restrain, imprison torture, drown, behead, kill and burn all kinds of specters and ghosts, the written charms are then burnt. Charms cure almost all diseases which erupt from the flesh, stomach-aches, headaches, stitches in the side, sore eyes. They cure sadness, fear and anxiety; they bring the departed souls, or if impossible, improve at least their condition in the "world of shades". Charms are also used to create a happy marriage, promoting harmony, love and understanding, between husband and wife. Charms have been used to invoke the goods to assist mankind, and to help overcome the influences of evil. For further reading visit the following website:http://witcheslore.com/bookofshadows/witches-workshop/charms-and-chinese-superstitions/3917/

- Do not cut your child's hair at night. It is believed that the witches/wizards will use the hair for witchcraft purposes. African Americans believe that you do not cut your baby's hair before his/her first birthday. It is assumed that if you do "hair" or bad luck. This could be true as African hair naturally changes consistency and texture many times throughout their lifetimes. The Chinese believe that clipping toenails or fingernails at night brings bad luck, as that person will be visited by ghosts. They further that a baby with more than one hair crown will be mischievous and disobedient. Indians believe that nails should not be cut at night for fear of evil spirits.

- Do not use a cup to drink water from a spring. The spring would dry up. You can use some tree leaves which you can convert into a cup or a gourd. It is normal to find a drinking gourd at the spring. The springs are usually found in the forest. It is believed that spiritual lions drink from such springs. Spiritual lions and spiritual mediums are conservative traditionalists who abhor western civilization.

- Working your field on Fridays is strictly prohibited. However, you can work your garden. Breaking this prohibition will result in prosecution at the chief's court. You never win this case. You are fined in the form of a goat. Refusal to pay the fine will result in the banishment from the chief's area of jurisdiction. Indians believe that Monday is not an auspicious for shaving and Thursday is a bad day for washing your hair. The day Friday is also significant in the western world. They believe that Friday the 13th is a very unlucky day especially for new beginnings. "The modern basis for the aura that surrounds Friday the 13th stems from Friday October the 13th, 1307. On this date, the Pope of the church in Rome in Conjunction with the King of France carried out a secret death warrant against "the Knights Templar". The Templers were terminated as heretics, never again to hold the power that they had held for so long. There Grand Master, Jacques

DeMolay, was arrested and before he was killed, was tortured and crucified. "The Chinese also associate the number 13 with bad luck. The number 13 has long been considered an unlucky number by the Egyptians and the ancient civilization. Some experts speculate that this was due to the fact that the people of the past knew how to count using only their 10 ten fingers and two feet which would up to a total maximum of 12.Thus after the number 12,the immediate next would be 13, was unknown and frightening to them. Even today, this number 13 is regarded as unlucky, note how most hotels do not have the 13th floor- the count goes from 12 to 14.

http://www.coolquiz.com/trivia/explain/docs/friday13.asp

• If a new daughter in-law drops and breaks her mother-inlaw's clay cooking pot on her first day in the family, it feels bad but that is a good omen as the new arrival is considered generous. She is held in high esteem. Americans have their different version of dropping something not necessarily concerning a daughter in-law. They believe that dropping and breaking a mirror spells bad luck to the perpetrator for the next seven years.

• Do not sweep your house during the night. It would mean you will chase away visitors and relatives. African Americans have a different version. They believe that do not allow children to sweep the floor, because they will invite unwanted guests.

- Hunters do not carry some salt in my local area. Salt is considered an unlucky product. It is believed that those who carry salt have a great appetite to eat meat, which will make the spirits angry. It is believed that the forests would not open up and you will not see any animals or catch any. However, some people believe that salt drives away witches/wizards. They toss salt in their houses at night. Americans believe that salt has always been considered a valuable substance capable of purifying and warding off evil spirits .By tossing salt over your left shoulder, you are driving away the evil spirits lurking with the intent to cause misfortune.

- My people associate the color red with loss of blood, or a funeral. It symbolizes sadness and sorrow. If you see a vehicle with a red tag it is a sign that the vehicle is carrying a dead person or the vehicles are in a funeral entourage. People put a red rag at their gate if there is a funeral or funeral vigil. The Zimbabwe flag has a red strip representing the blood lost during the war of liberation. The Chinese believe to the contrary. The Chinese believe that the color red is a color of good luck. During the Chinese Lunar New Year , married Chinese would give their children, friends and relatives red packets filled with money as a symbol of good luck, as the color red symbolizes fire which is used to scare away evil spirits.

Legends

There are several legends in Zimbabwe. These include among others, Chaminuka, Mbuya Nehanda, and Nyaminyami, Six to Six Snake, Mount Nyanga, Sekuru Kaguvi and many others. The free encyclopedia defines a legend as a narrative of human actions that are perceived both by teller and listeners to take place within human history and to possess certain qualities that give the tale verisimilitude.Chamiuka was a Shona prophet who had immense spiritual powers. It is believed that he tamed such creatures such as pythons and other snakes, antelopes, kudu, and other game species. He was credited for bringing rain. He prophesied the coming of the white man to then Southern Rhodesia (Zimbabwe).He played a spiritual role during the Zimbabwe war of liberation. Sadly he was killed near Shangani River by Lobengula, the Ndebele king on false accusations. To read more about the legend Chaminuka visit the following website http://chirandu.blogspot.com/2007/06/chaminuka.html.

Mbuya Nehanda (Charwe Nyakasikana)_was a powerful woman spirit medium that was committed to upholding traditional Shona culture; she was instrumental in organizing the nationwide resistance to colonial rule during the First Chimurenga of 1896-7.

She colluded in the resistance with such renowned spirit mediums as Skekuru Kaguvi (Gumboreshumba), chief Mashayamombe, and others. Even Lobengula the Ndebele King recognized her as a powerful spiritual medium in the land. She and Sekuru Kaguvi were accused in the murder of a brutal British South Africa Company Commissioner a Mr. Henry Hawkins Pollard in theMazowe area. It is believed thatMbuya Nehanda and Sekuru Kaguvi were tried at the Old Franch South Africa Company building which was demolished to make way for the elegant Reserve Bank of Zimbabwe building. The presiding judge was Judge Watermeyer while Mr. Henry Castens was the acting prosecutor .Mbuya Nehanda and Sekuru Kaguvi were sentence to the gallows. It is believed that they were both hanged on a "Musasa" tree in Josiah Tongogara Avenue. However, before she was hanged a Roman Catholic Priest Richartz was sent to convert her into Christianity but she refused to talk to him and she asked to be taken back to her people in Mazowe. Both were hanged on April 27, 1898. That "Musasa" tree became an icon of the Zimbabwe Liberation Struggle. It commanded a lot of respect among the black community. It is believed that there were numerous car accidents involving the tree. Legend says that the tree was never damaged but most of the cars involved were "right offs." However, a Wedensday, 12/07/2011 Harare City Council employees were repairing the tarmac at the corner of Josiah Tongogara Avenue and Sam Nujoma Street accidentally knocked down the "Musasa"tree that stood in the middle of the road. It is said that upon releasing the tragedy the culprits ran away in fear of the reprisals from the ancestral spirit of the legend Mbuya Nehanda.

For more information about Mbuya Nehanda visit the following website http://www.bulawayo1872.com/history/nehandambuya. htm

MOUNT NYANGA

It is rather preposterous to talk about Nyanga District without mentioning the legend Rekayi Tangwena. Chief Rekayi Tangwena resisted the then Prime Minister of Rhodesia Ian Smith's machinations to relocate him from his spiritual fatherland of Gaeresi to the arid Gokwe District in the west of the country. The idea was to turn Gaeresi into a dairy farm. However, that project never took place. Chief Tangwena and his people stayed put. Ian Smith regime razed his and his subjects' houses using bulldozers. Chief Tangwena never fought back but offered passive resistance. Tangwena ran into the forests and mountains, and hills. Some of the people crossed the border into independent Mozambique. As soon as the regime soldiers left Chief Tangwena and his came back and constructed plastic shelters defying all odds to leave. Some of children were taken away from their parents and placed in Children's Homes to force compliance but that did not deter Chief Tangwena and his people. The resistance is akin to that of the Cherokees who refused to be relocated across the Mississippi to Oklahoma and other reservations in the west. That kind of résistance became a symbol of bravery and courage to fight the Zimbabwe revolutionary war. Chief Rekayi Tangwena helped the armed revolutionary leaders like President Mugabe and Edgar Tekere cross the Rhodesian border into Mozambique. Chief Tangwena later crossed the border into Mozambique and helped the revolution fighters with his knowledge of the Nyanga terrain and his spiritual prowess. He gave counsel to the revolutionary fighters and political leaders. Chief Rekayi Tangwena returned to independent Zimbabwe and became part of the Government. He is now buried at the National Heroes Acre in Harare. Chief Rekayi Tangwena's name resonates with the homeless who construct plastic structures in urban. Such squatter settlements are known as "Tangwenas.," as symbol of resistance, bravery and perseverance.

*Mount Nyanga: Disrespectful people
could disappear without any trace.*

Mount Nyanga(formerly Mount in Inyangani) is the highest mountain in Zimbabwe standing at 2592 meters(8504 feet).It is situated within Nyanga National Park in Nyanga District The summit of Mount Nyanga lies atop a small outcrop of rock around 40 meters above the surrounding area. The remainder of the peak is broad moor of mainly rolling and plateau with an area of about 8 square kilometers. The edges of this of this plateau then fall steeply to east and west side.

Locals believe that Mount Nyanga has the ability to vanish people especially children. Scores of people have disappeared without trace. Two girls from Widdecombe Elementary School in Harare disappeared while on a field trip. Locals believe that Mount Nyanga has the ability to suck and initiate the disappearance of those with foul mouths who speak against the mountain, its people, fauna and flora. It is advisable to enlist the services of tour guides who are always available at the ascending points. Scientists believe that since it rains nearly every day the soils are saturated with water, it develops into quick sands. Therefore people who stray from the marked foot paths may be sucked in by the quick sands. There is no scientific proof that Mount Nyanga has the ability to vanish people. However, science and superstition are not compatible. There is no need to educate the locals on the second theory of quick sands.

The mountain can be accessed from four base points within Nyanga National Park:

1. The official car park, at the base of the Tourist Route. This is reached from Circular Drive.

2. The Mountain Club of Zimbabwe hut, on the Kwaraguza Road, accessed via Circular Drive.

3. Nyazengu Substation of Nyanga National Park, accessed via a road which goes south from just before the official car park.

4. Gleneagles Substation of Nyanga National Park, accessed via the Circular Drive, Kwaraguza Road and the Gleneagles road or fromTroutbeck via Nyafaru

Sacred Snake entering Mazowe Dam.

NYAMINYAMI

WozzaWorks (2003-2012) gave the following accurate narrative of Nyaminyami the River God. "He has a body like a snake and a head like a fish and no one knows how big he is, for he never showed himself in full display. The people of Zambezi Valley in Zimbabwe were protected by Nyaminyami, their ancestral spirit (Mudzimu), who fed them from his own

Nyaminyami the River God Sculpture.

meat in times of hunger. The people pledged their allegiance to him by performing ceremonial dances.

For many years Nyaminyami and his wife stayed safely at Kariba, the spot which was their home and near that spot, that's where it all began. One season when Nyaminyami's wife had gone down the mighty Kariwa Gorge to other people of the Valley to answer their prayers and bless her people, the white man came to build a wall.

It took five long years to see it through because Nyaminyami did not want to be disturbed. He caused some floods and loss of life, but at last he was kind enough to let the wall to be all complete. It is also believed that the occasional earth tremor felt in the lake surroundings is caused by this spirit.

It was the work of the Tonga elders and their medium spirits to persuade the Nyaminyami to allow the Zambezi to be tamed. But Shame! Nyaminyami was separated from his wife.

Great bodies of water are considered sacred, for water is essential for the life of the village in an often arid land. Wherever there is water, the Africans find prosperity. The Nyaminyami is the ruler of water and his symbol is worn to ward off the forces of darkness and to attract wealth." Nyaminyami, the legend is symbolized on a walking stick which most locals take pride as one of their possessions. Tourists also buy the walking stick as a souvenir

Each part of the Nyaminyami walking stick represents something.

Nyaminyami Walking Stick

Source: WozzaWorks 2003-2012

The Handle: Represents "Nyaminyami" who the Tonga people believe is their spirit god and that the occasional earth tremor felt in the lake surroundings is caused by this spirit.

The Tree: Mopani tree which is found in the Zambezi Valley, the Spirals represent the waves on the Zambezi River; the fish is representative of the staple food of the Tonga people, who prior to the building of Kariba Dam, fished daily on the Zambezi River.

The Figures: represents people on the Zambezi River banks during their ceremonial dances.

The Wooden Rings: represents the bangles worn by the Tonga women as a decoration during the ceremonial dances.

The Sign of the Hand: represents the holding of the "Magical Ball" used by the Tonga fortune tellers to guard against evil spirits.

Women's Bubble Pipe: is normally a long calabash and is used to by the Tonga people for smoking tobacco. In the past these pipes were used to for smoking "dagga" – a Tonga tradition.

Legend says that an ancestral snake took twelve hours (6.00 am to6.00 pm) to cross the Harare-Bindura road into Mazowe Dam from an adjacent mountain causing a traffic stretching miles on each side of the road. Drivers would not dare run over it as doing so could have brought a bad omen to themselves and their families. It is taboo to kill an ancestral animal such as a snake, lion, leopard, and many others.Noone could ascertain where its tail and head were. People from as far as Harare, nearby farms, and a nearby High school rushed to see the spectacle. It is prohibited to take pictures of anything of ancestral phenomenon. People just described how it looked .Therefore they were different versions on its color and size. It is said it changed its color from time to time hence different color and size versions. It is said that even white commercial farmers who were oblivious to the African culture and religion came to see for themselves. It said that they bought some black and white pieces of cloth to appease the African medium spirits. Failure to appease the spirits could have brought some devastating consequences to farming businesses. Ancestral spirits are capable of instructing lions, leopards, hyenas and other predators to kill their cattle, sheep and goats. Ancestral spirits could cause droughts, or introduce pests like swarms of army worms or locusts. The Mazowe area was home to the revolutionary icon Mbuya Nehanda earlier own alluded to in this contribution. The six to six was believed to be a revelation of future things to come- the armed revolution.Mbuya Nehanda warned the white man before they hanged and killed her that her " bones were going to rise" and reclaim the land taken by the colonialists.

http://www.flickr.com/photos/rickinzim/4099353733/in/photostream/

In conclusion superstitions and myths are generally rooted in each and every society. Some superstitions and myths are generational and dynamic. Some superstitions go off the social radar but still new ones come. We do not know exactly who creates them but we see them in our social fabric. Superstitions are different from society to society, community to community and country to country. We do not have to question other people's beliefs but respect them. There is no scientific proof on each superstition to authenticate its relevance, but here we are stuck in the world of superstitions. We have to respect them as they are engrained on us from the cradle to the grave. Some people may try to ignore superstitions in public but secretly they acknowledge them. Some superstitions are educational while others are mere speculations. We may ignore superstitions at our own peril because we may be socially stigmatized if we speak publicly against them. We do not lose much by joining the social band wagon and accept them although in our private lives we may chose to accommodate those that are compliant to our beliefs. Legends and myths are usually icons of strengths, courage, and bravery. Some legends are factual while others are fairy tales; however, they both serve the same purpose- to inspire us. We have to believe legends and myths as they are. I have observed that no matter our academic achievements we believe in certain things which do have any scientific proof. Religion is one those things we believe in but at a closer look there is no proof that certain things actually happened.

References

New Zimbabwe Newspaper (2009) Naked Basket Flight Woman –Witch. http://www.newzimbabwe.com/pages/witchcraft7.19898.html.

IOL Newspaper (2009) Naked "Witches" to Face Trial. http://www.iol.co.za/news/africa/naked-witches-to-face-trial-1.1330309

BBC News Witch Burning in Kenya

news.bbc.co.uk/2/hi/Africa/8119201.stm

New Zimbabwe Newspaper. Zimbabwe Outlaws Practice of Witchcraft. http://www.newzimbabwe.com/pages/witchcraft2.14064.html

Unusual Trivia Collection. http://www.corsinet.com/trivia/scary.html

Rain Dreams Meaning. http://www.dreamsleep.net/rain-dream-meaning.html

Fire Dream Meaning. http://www.dreamsleep.net/meaning-of-fire-dream.html

Puddle in Dream: Dictionary Meaning and Symbol. http://www.experienceproject.com/dream-dictionary/Puddle-dreams

The MOB Eating. http://www.youtube.com/watch?v=h_4MCKL6kcg

That Explains It. http://www.coolquiz.com/trivia/explain/docs/friday13.asp

Mutsiwemvura: Chaminuka. http://chirandu.blogspot.com/2007/06/chaminuka.html.

http://chirandu.blogspot.com/2007/06/chaminuka.html.

The History of Mbuya Nehanda http://www.bulawayo1872.com/history/nehandambuya.html

The Story of Nyaminyami. http://www.wozzaworks.com/nyaminyami.asp

Mount Nyanga. http://en.wikipedia.org/wiki/Mount_Nyangani

Native American Superstition and Religion. http://www.nanations.com/jesuits/religion_superstitions.htm

Myths Revealed: The Origin of Common Superstitions http://www.lifescript.com/soul/spirit/beliefs/10_common_superstitions.aspx?gclid=CNGQiOWHq7ECFQbonAod_hAA4g&trans=1&du=1&ef_id=S7lozNBbriUAAGRlFDkAAATA%3a20120721151545%3as

North American Superstitions. http://www.superstitionsof.com/north-american-superstitions.htm

10 Common Superstitions. http://www.lifescript.
com/soul/spirit/beliefs/10_common_superstitions.
aspx?gclid=CNGQiOWHq7ECFQbonAod_
hAA4g&trans=1&du=1&ef_id=S7lozNBbriUAAGRlFDkAAA
TA%3a20120721151545%3as

Ancient Civilization. http://library.thinkquest.org/C004203/
religion/religion05.htm

Chinese Dream Dictionary. http://www.absolutelyfengshui.com/
others/dreams-dictionary-1.php

Dreams: http://www.springsgreetingcards.com/catalogs/store.
asp?pid=234180&catid=22647

Witchcraft. http://www.witchcraftandwitches.com/world_asia.
html

Dark Side of India: Witchcraft and Superstition. http://www.
newstrackindia.com/newsdetails/3032

The Hidden Meaning of Dreams. http://www.psychics.co.uk/
blog/dreams/

Charms and Chinese Superstition. http://witcheslore.com/
bookofshadows/witches-workshop/charms-and-chinese-
superstitions/3917/

The Meat: Lawful and Unlawful in Islam. http://www.azhar.jp/
info/halal-eng/halal6.html

The Biblical Prohibition from Eating Blood. http://www.contra-
mundum.org/schirrmacher/eating_blood.pdf

Meat: Is veal production crueler than other forms of meat. http://
www.quora.com/Meat/Is-veal-production-crueler-than-with-
other-forms-of-meat

Some Superstitions About Food Shouldn't Be Dismissed
as Myth. http://articles.sun-sentinel.com/1986-07-23/
features/8602130068_1_hot-water-spinach-fever

Health Benefits of Okra http://thoughtstoliveby.wordpress.
com/2009/08/17/health-benefits-of-okra/

More Gardening Superstitions: Fruit and Veggie Tales. http://
voices.yahoo.com/more-gardening-superstitions-fruit-veggie-
tales-519285.html?cat=32

www.ingramcontent.com/pod-product-compliance
Lightning Source LLC
Chambersburg PA
CBHW020403290526
45785CB00005B/2427